PURPOSE OF

PRAISE

(Six Biblical Reasons Why We Praise)

by

Andrew Allans Mutambo

PURPOSE OF PRAISE

Unless otherwise noted, all scripture quotations are from the
original King James Version of the Bible.

Rivendell Publishing

www.rivendellpublishing.com

To order copies online visit:

Andrewmutambo.com

Or by mail contact:

Pastor Andrew Mutambo

P.O BOX 22292

Kampala, Uganda.

U.S (Google line): 1-804-601-0394. Ugandan

(Mobile line) : +256-772-404389 Email:

andymutts@gmail.com

Layout desgin: Elohe Enterprise Designs

Table of Contents

Dedication

I owe everything about this book to the great King and Father of all, for the grace and inspiration about worship that He has put on my heart for my generation.

In addition, my parents have been my role models from a tender age. Dad has always encouraged me to go higher, while Mum has often been the soft spoken prophet in my life. Thank you, dad and mum, for the nurturing work you have done in me. Most of the principles you taught me are still sustaining me to this day. I dedicate this book to you as well.

For all who chance to read this book, may the good Lord awaken and stir your heart to deeper dimensions of Praise. Let the King of glory rejoice over you with singing.

Acknowledgements

Once again my fellow Pastors' of Revived Glory Church, thank you for your continuous encouragement, love, prayers, and for allowing me to pursue this dream and its authorial formulation. And to my Church family, my sincere gratitude for your love, support and patience during the times of separation and study in the course of writing my books. You are the wind beneath my wings.

Thanks to Bill Jackson of Charlottesville, Virginia, USA for editing my manuscript.

Introduction

The word 'Praise' in the Bible (King James Version) first appears in the book of Genesis when Leah, one of Jacob's wives, gives birth to Judah. She exclaims, 'Now will I praise the Lord'. From that moment, throughout scripture, it is used with diverse applications. The Hebraic Old testament uses a variety of words to define Praise. The most commonly used are: (1) Barak, to kneel and bless God as an act of adoration; (2) Hillul, a celebration or thanksgiving to God for a harvest, (3) Halal, to make a show, to boast, to be clamorously foolish for God, (4) Zamar, to make music accompanied by a voice, to celebrate in song and music, (5) Yadah, to revere or worship God with extended hands, (6) Mahalal, to praise God for his fame, (7) Shabach, to address in a loud tone/voice in glory and commendation, and (8) Tehillah, laudation/extolling God specifically in a hymn.

Friends, these different avenues of praise as practiced

by the Jewish people offer us a comprehensive 'praise-package' that can help us access God and present to him the best sacrifice of our praise. Hebrews 13:15 By him therefore let us offer the sacrifice of praise to God continually, that is, the fruit of our lips giving thanks to his name. One should also take note that there is an instituted protocol for accessing and meeting with the King.

Psalms 100:4 Enter into his gates with thanksgiving, and into his courts with praise: be thankful unto him, and bless his name.

While making your way through the gates and courts of the palace to meet with your King, your gate-pass (Praise) is pre-loaded with power, potential and immense benefits that will accrue from its usage. Praise is one of the greatest kinds of machinery availed to kingdom Citizens. The book of Psalms is awash with numerous examples and case scenarios from its practice. It documents the life and struggles of David before and after he became king of Israel. It cites many examples including the time he was on the run from King Saul, his beckoning calls of prayer and seasons of praise for God's faithfulness, mercy and deliverance.

Praise has been known to bolster the hearts of those who have grown weary. It is the music of our soul and fruit of our lips. It is a divine tree planted in us by God; whenever we praise, God feeds! Praise is meant to be an inherent practice of everything with breath. Scripture records 'let everything that hath breath praise the Lord'. It is the starter course on God's menu, we being His waitresses. Praise is also a declaration of His kingdom rule and influence on earth. Whenever we engage in a praise spree we are making public to the principalities and powers that the Kingdoms of this world are under the rule and influence of Jehovah God. It is also a celebration of His victories in our lives, past, present and future. The Bible attests to God showing up when His people praised him. Praise liberates the soul and creates the atmosphere for a divine encounter. It is a power shifter and a propellant to your place of freedom. Praise knows no barriers of race, gender, age and social status. It is a universal practice of every Child of God.

In this book, I come looking at it via a different angle.

I share with you the purpose of praise. While scripture commands us to praise, we also see the mammoth benefits coming from it. My assignment is to take you to the heart and well spring of it. When you discover the reason why you ought to praise, the results will speak for themselves. In the subsequent chapters, I spell out the six biblical reasons why we praise. It is my prayer that when done reading this book, your understanding and perception of praise will be revolutionized, lifting you to a higher level of citizenship in the Kingdom. God loves and honors a people that praise Him. Psalms 22:3 And thou art holy, thou that dwellest amid the praises of Israel. (Darby Bible).

Chapter One

FOR HIS WORD

Through the ages, the Word of God has been and still is the greatest spiritual tool of the Church. It has been criticized, ostracized, misused, treaded on and even burnt, with the hope of making it extinct. But it has endured and still remains the only credible document that sheds light on the will, purpose, plan and design of God for every unborn, living and dead person. It is encoded with set bounds and seasons for all nations and kingdoms past, present and future. It is also the foremost asset for a Christian in accessing the voice of God.

In the Kingdom of God, His Word is Law. He rules, governs and administrates by it. Everything that was created is a product of His Word. Hebrews 11:3 Through faith we understand that the worlds were framed by the word of God, so that things which are seen were not made of things which do appear. Everything God does comes through proclamation. He speaks it into being. Whether it is your healing, deliverance, protection, etc. Psalms 107:20 He sent his word, and healed them, and delivered them from their destructions.

Therefore, we His kingdom citizens emulate our King by creating a wholesome 'world' around us as we declare His word in every circumstance of our lives. The Word of God is two (bits?) in one; the Written Word (commonly called the Bible) AND the Living Word (the Eternal Christ). Before the express or written Word was, the Living Word was. That is why in heaven Christ is referred to as the Word of God.

Revelation 19:11 And I saw heaven opened, and behold a white horse; and he that sat upon him was called Faithful and True, and in righteousness he doth judge and make war.

Revelation 19:12 His eyes were as a flame of fire, and on his head were many crowns; and he had a name written, that no man knew, but he himself.

Revelation 19:13 And he was clothed with a vesture dipped in blood: and his name is called The Word of God.

The written Word, also Known as Logos, is a product of God. Logos means 'reason and logic'. It is His reason and thinking about Man and the universe, His voice through the eons of time. It carries the breath of His Eternal Spirit upon it. You cannot separate the Living Logos from the written logos; because the latter is a product of the former.

John 6:63 It is the spirit that quickeneth; the flesh profiteth nothing: the words that I speak unto you, they are spirit, and they are life.

Having said that, His written Word gives us insight as to why we praise. Let us examine the following scripture.

Psalms 56:10 In God will I praise his word: in the LORD will I praise his word.

The Psalmist offers a remarkable key to our praises. He tells us to Praise His Word. There are several reasons for doing this. The elevated status or position of His Word in Heaven makes it impregnable and supreme. No one can break through it, corrupt it, not even manipulate it. The scripture says, it is forever settled (erected, established, made to stand upright and appointed) in heaven. (Psalms 119:89). It occupies a position of supreme authority and rank in the heavens. Its legitimacy and faithfulness make it a dependable anchor. The Word of God does not change NOR can it be altered. That is why you and I can refer to it, reflect on it, rehearse and release it into the different areas of our lives with utmost surety.

Isaiah 55:11 So shall my word be that goeth forth out of my mouth: it shall not return unto me void, but it shall accomplish that which I please, and it shall prosper in the thing whereto I sent it.

Mathew 24:35 Heaven and earth shall pass away, but my words shall not pass away.

2 Corinthians 1:20 For all the promises of God in him are yea, and in him Amen, unto the glory of God by us.

Additionally, its surgical precision makes it a transformer as it works its way into our bodies, soul and spirit; and while doing so, like an anti-fungal OR anti-bacterial, it begins inflicting harm and destruction upon every diabolic work and influence. When you and I take time to listen, read, meditate and apply it into our lives, it automatically goes to work by healing, transforming, delivering, restoring and renewing us, leaving our 'houses' clean and garnished, free of any demonic activity that has pitched camp therein. It also begins ferrying and fetching all the wonderful goods that our heavenly father wills for us: health, joy, prosperity, protection, long life and favor!

Folks, we have every reason to praise God for His Word. However, it is important to know it. How else would you bask in it? As we praise (boast, shout, dance and sing) in/for it, rehearsing it over every situation, God hears, is compelled to crash the party AND make things happen for our good. There is nothing that captivates God like declaring His Word to him. How much more if you do it through your praises. He enjoys it more when He receives a 'return-parcel' of His word, wrapped in your Praises. He is bound to respond faster. It is time to wrap the Word in your praises, flavored with a grateful and expectant heart. It is one of your most viable keys to victorious living!

Chapter Two

FOR HIS NAME

History past and present has produced some of the most captivating names in a variety of fields. Allow me talk about the ones about which I am more keen. In the politic arena, we have had the likes of Nelson Mandela, a great leader and Icon highly revered by the South African people. He is called Papa meaning 'father'. In the religious field we have Mother Theresa, a woman of Indian origin, who with her beliefs mothered many orphans and helpless children giving them a sense of purpose and helping them know they were formed in God's image and are dear to Him. In the academic world, we have had the likes Albert Einstein, often regarded as the father of modern physics, who discovered the law of photo-electric effect thereby changing the face of that science. These names and countless more have come and some gone, but the greatest and most powerful of all, is the name of Jesus, given to him by God, through the Angel Gabriel; before he was even conceived OR born.

Raised as a son of a carpenter, in an insignificant northern coastal town of Nazareth, He was later to become the Savior of the world. His early years were silent until He was called into ministry at the age of thirty. He was rejected and condemned to die by the very people He came to save. Was crucified, died and rose from the grave the third day, just as He foretold, the only being that was able to conquer death and hell.

He now sits at the right hand of His Majesty, highly exalted, far above all powers, kingdoms and thrones. He has been given a name that is above ALL names. At the mention of His name, every knee will bow and tongue will confess He is Lord. Whereas other names have faded with time, His has continuously resounded through the pages of history and will be there till close of the ages. In this second chapter, we discover another reason as to why we praise.

Psalms 54:6 I will freely sacrifice unto thee: I will praise thy name, O LORD; for it is good.

If we were to unearth the enormity of reasons for praising His name, it would take more editions of this book. Nevertheless, let me give you some that will compel you to make a self discovery. The name of Jesus is a gate-pass that warrants us unlimited access to the eternal God, wherever and whenever. God be praised that He has given us a 'stress code,' the shortest prayer and hotline to Heaven. Whosoever shall call upon the name of the Lord shall be saved. In a Christian's vocabulary, the name of Jesus is the most used word. When approaching and fellowshipping with the father, we do it through the name of Jesus; because it is the only one heaven has mandated for this purpose. He has allowed us to utilize it 24/7 and is always ready to listen.

John 16:24 Hitherto have ye asked nothing in my name: ask, and ye shall receive, that your joy may be full.

It is also pre-loaded with wealth, power, healing and deliverance at its invocation. The name of the Lord carries a wide variety of properties that come afloat when vocalized. The book of Acts sheds light on its application and the results that ensue. Peter and John are on their way to the temple, at the hour of prayer. They find a man seated at the gate called Beautiful. When he asks them for money, they tell him, Silver and gold we have none, but in the name of Jesus, rise and walk. The paralytic rises, leaps and follows them into the temple. The whole place is thrown in a frenzy seeing the man who always sat by the gate, jumping, leaping and praising God in the temple.

Another incident happens when Paul and Silas in the City of Philippi are encountered by a girl with a spirit of divination. For a while, she had followed them as a fortune-teller, telling people who they were. Agitated and weary of her proclamations, Paul turns and commands the spirit to come out of her, in the name of Jesus. She is instantly delivered.

Half way through the ministry of Jesus, the disciples are assigned in twos to go preach the gospel in the different towns and villages of Israel. They return joyfully to their Master (Jesus) saying, the demons are subject to us in Your name. He tells them rather to rejoice because their names are written in heaven. We can go on and on citing scriptural examples of the operations of His name and perhaps quote our own life experiences. The important thing is knowing what a mine of wealth it is, a reservoir!

His name is an impenetrable fortress for his people; whose excellence reverberates in all spheres. The writer of the book of Proverbs says 'the name of the Lord is a strong tower, the righteous run into it and they are safe'. It's a garrison for the Christian. When invoked in times of trouble, it immediately becomes our fortified bunker. When under its influence, there is no demon in hell that can touch us, simply because it was given overwhelming status above every other name AND at its mention every knee bows and every tongue confesses that Jesus is Lord.

Folks, the evidence I have advanced should awaken and stir you to celebrate His name through your praises, because of its value and benefits. A further look at the verses below explains why you should praise His name. The Psalmist tells us to praise His name because it is excellent'. The biblical definition of excellent is, 'has been set up on high, lofty and is exalted'. The writer of the book of songs goes on to proclaim His name as a perfume poured forth. Did you know that whenever you sing praises about His name, the fragrance that is embedded within it begins oozing out and, coming through your lips, God smells it and becomes engrossed in your praises?

Psalms 148:13 Let them praise the name of the LORD: for his name alone is excellent; his glory is above the earth and heaven.

Songs of Solomon 1:3 Sweet is the smell of your perfumes; your name is as perfume running out; so the young girls give you their love. (1965 Bible in Basic English).

Beloved, if we learn to praise His name for its properties (as mentioned above), we will accomplish far more than we could via our petitions, **because praise is prayer in multiples.** When you begin elevating it, He will use it to elevate you. Let us take hold of the name of Jesus and begin doing some 'Barak' with it!

Chapter Three

For His Power

From ages past, the quest for 'power' has been a cutting edge issue. The first documentation of such an act is in heaven when Lucifer craves the seat and position of God. Isaiah 14:13 For thou hast said in thine heart, I will ascend into heaven, I will exalt my throne above the stars of God: I will sit also upon the mount of the congregation, in the sides of the north: Isaiah 14:14 I will ascend above the heights of the clouds; I will be like the most High. Scripture tells us what the repercussions were. He was cast out of heaven marking the beginning of his eternal fall and doom. However, this satanic ambition was passed on to fallen Man and through the ages many have fallen prey to its snare.

The holy scriptures vividly tell us that God is the source and embodiment of power. The same power oozes from Him to fulfill His divine purpose. When Abraham is promised a Son and a nation from his bowels, he is at a stage in life where humanly speaking, his aged body and that of Sarah cannot deliver. Genesis 17:1 tells us, And when Abram was ninety years old and nine, the LORD appeared to Abram, and said unto him, I am the Almighty God; walk before me, and be thou perfect." God underscored His sovereignty to Abraham as the El-Shaddai, the all sufficient and having all sufficiency, the power to make happen whatever and whenever!

God is the Master and Ruler of everything. The universe is a product of His creation. He has creation rights over you, me and everything. That credits Him with power. Jeremiah 51:15 He hath made the earth by his power, he hath established the world by his wisdom, and hath stretched out the heaven by his understanding. Regenerate Man, those bought back by the saving grace of Christ, have been granted ruler-ship and management over His possessions. We are privileged to have a father who owns everything and is willing to elevate and distribute to His children as He wills. Job 36:22 Behold, God exalteth by his power: who teacheth like him?

That said, we are not going to muse over Who He is and what He Has. We should go beyond that by discovering how to tap into this 'Power'. Scripture helps to clue us in.

Psalms 21:13 Be thou exalted, LORD, in thine own strength: so will we sing and praise thy power.

Lets read again what the Psalmist says in the second part of the verse, 'so will we sing and praise your power'. Wow, that is it! We are told to sing and praise His power. The psalmist from the opening verses of Psalm 21 advances several reasons for doing this. He mentions how God has given him his heart's desire and has not withheld the request of his lips; how He has given him a crown of gold, given him life and length of days. Has blessed him forever and made him most glad. These among others were the reasons David sang and praised God for his power.

Correspondingly, you and I have seen and experienced the hand of God in different areas. Throughout your lifetime, you ought to write and sing your own Psalm about His power. When we praise God for His power, we are provoking Him to arise to our help and crush our enemies. Do not forget that **praise is a declaration to the principalities and powers of our King's rule and dominion.** In these moments of praise-declaration, He is aroused, steps in and begins flexing His muscle over every bondage and foot hold of the devil in your life. As the LORD of Hosts and commander in Chief of His forces, He is ever present when His 'praise-force' begins trumpeting their praises to Him. He is stirred up as a 'Man out of sleep' and begins confusing and annihilating the enemy forces. Jeremiah 32:27 Behold, I am the LORD, the God of all flesh: is there anything too hard for me? Psalms 66:7 He ruleth by his power for ever; his eyes behold the nations: let not the rebellious exalt themselves. Selah.

No more time to lose. This evening before you retire and tomorrow morning as you rise, begin praising Him for the unseen force (power) that sustains you and protects you through the day. Start from there and sing your own psalm, a daily diary of praises concerning His power. As you fill your heart with these wonderful thoughts and words, only you and God will recount the proceeds.

- **Praise is a disposition of your soul; notice, "Will I Praise..."**

Chapter Four

For His Works

From generation to generation, God has demonstrated His mercy, grace and love to countless nations and peoples. One of the most captivating stories is the one of the children of Israel. After the demise of the patriarchs Abraham, Isaac and Jacob, their descendants, the children of Israel are forced to settle in Egypt because of famine. They begin to multiply so rapidly that the Egyptians are threatened by their numbers. A new Pharaoh comes on the scene who knows nothing about Joseph, and subjects the race to slavery, rigorous bondage and servitude. For over 400 years this goes on.

The Hebrews began raising beckoning calls to God for deliverance. In the fullness of time their cries come into the ears of God and He sends a deliverer in the person of Moses. We all know how with a strong hand, diverse miracles, signs and wonders He brings them out of Egypt, through the red-sea and blistering wilderness to the promised land. A journey of forty years. This story is also a reflection of a Christian's journey of life and the hurdles faced on the way to the 'promised land'.

It is important to note that the works of God are a testament of His unchanging-ness and willingness to reach forth. It is the nature of God to be merciful and gracious. Even when we are unfaithful, He remains faithful. People of all ages irrespective of their beliefs have raised beckoning calls to their Maker and He has come to their rescue as it deemed Him fit. Notwithstanding, it carries more weight when His children, those who have come to love and accept Him as King and Lord, look to Him. He doubtless hears and comes to our rescue. And because of His acts, successive generations praise Him and declare His mighty works. Let us see what the Bible says about it.

Psalms 145:4 One generation shall praise thy works to another, and shall declare thy mighty acts.

Folks, remembering and rehearsing these acts of God in our lives through the lens of scripture is vital. We are instructed to praise God for His acts in our respective generations. Some of these doings may have occurred before we were even born OR while alive but had no control over them. I will cite an example of one of the most ruthless dictators of my time, Idi Amin, who ruled my nation of Uganda from 1971 to 1979. I happened to be alive but very young, unable to know or influence the course of events. I know only through my parents and elderly folk about the gross murders, witchcraft and persecution of Christians that was rampant during his tenure. The church went underground, the economy declined and the nation was on the verge of collapse. His goal was to turn our nation into an Islamic state. The cries of my fellow Ugandans, the prayers and fasting of the Church and above all God's unending mercy brought about an end to Idi Amin's regime. Looking back many years after, am compelled to praise God for His acts of mercy and goodness over my nation. Frankly, am not sure I would be alive today if events had continued the way they were.

Deuteronomy 16:12   And thou shalt remember that

thou wast a bondman in Egypt: and thou shalt observe and do these statutes.

Deuteronomy 16:13 Thou shalt observe the feast of tabernacles seven days, after that thou hast gathered in thy corn and thy wine:

Psalms 107:8 Oh that men would praise the LORD for his goodness, and for his wonderful works to the children of men!

Isaiah 38:19 The living, the living, he shall praise thee, as I do this day: the father to the children shall make known thy truth.

I may not know much about your nation, community and family. However, I do know that there are many things in our lives which, if they had not been averted or stopped, would have had a negative multiplier effect on our present lives. It is imperative to praise God for His works in your life, your family, your nation, your city and your universe. Imagine the continuous news we hear about meteorites and alien bodies wanting to crash into our planet and by a whisker they flash by. If they had impacted the earth, the damage and loss would have been enormous. Do you reckon all this happens by accident? I suppose not. It is time that we wake up and recognize the mercy, grace and goodness of God to us His creation.

Imagine those living in war prone, earthquake prone, Tsunami prone areas and severe conditions of life around the world; living another day may be a miracle to them. Again, picture the hustle of traffic you have to go through to get to your work place/school and back; it is horrific. We are often accident prone. And for those of you who have to catch periodic flights for work, business and pleasure it is more mind-boggling. Have you ever sat back, taken a deep breath and said, 'Thank you, Lord, for your mighty acts of love that I may not deserve BUT are made available to me because of your mercy and goodness'.

Friend, am challenging and inspiring you to get perspective. Nothing in life should be taken for granted; from the free volumes of air you breath in to the constant skirmishes of life you go through scratch free OR bruised, yet always salvaged by the merciful hand of God. Learn to praise Him for His works in your life (whatever is around you and in your generation).

Chapter Five

For His Avenging

Have you gotten a chance to 'walk' into the greatest library of all time, the Bible. Have you taken time to pick from its shelves and read any or all of the sixty six books therein. Well, these books give documented accounts of the amazing display of God's hand of vengeance. A good chunk is about His people, the nation of Israel and scattered individual figures who sought Him in times of trouble. It is astonishing how He often showed up and avenged them of their enemies. Let us peek into one of the books and see how applicable this is to our subject.

Judges 5:2 Praise ye the LORD for the avenging of Israel, when the people willingly offered themselves.

This was the time of the judges, before Israel got a

king. God used to raise individual persons to govern and lead His people. Notice how Deborah and Barak burst into song saying, 'Praise the Lord for avenging Israel His people'. If you follow the story from the preceding chapter, you will discover that there had been a continuing battle between the tribes of Israel and the Canaanites who had mightily oppressed them for twenty years. God raises a deliverer in the person of Barak under the guidance of Deborah, a Prophetess. He assembles an army of ten thousand men from the different tribes and marches in battle against this overwhelming Canaanite force. The archives record that God discomfited and decimated the vast Canaanite army before General Barak and the end result was emancipation from the tyrannical rule. This led to an outburst of celebration by the key leaders Deborah and Barak, echoing the power of God.

This episode throws significant light on one of the 'whys' of our praise. We praise God for His avenging. It is amazing how often times God fights for us in plain sight and at other times behind the scenes; always getting us victories over our foes. As I have said, some battles may be seen with our naked eye and others obscured from us for our good; yet in all, as a loving father and caring King, He never allows the enemy to fulfill his purpose.

You and I will never fully comprehend the magnitude of our enemies' wrath AND God's mercies during these continuous battles of life, how He often fights for our lives, spouses, children, careers, health, education, ministries and destiny. When the battle(s) is over, we are avenged and our enemies left wallowing in defeat. Because He said, 'I will never leave you nor forsake you'. If you and I take stock of our lives, we will discover that there have been moments when Satan's attacks have found us exposed, on the opposite side of God's grace, but because of His unending mercy, He has guarded and guided us safely in His arms, with victory in our hands.

Let us pick another book from the library and look at one of the stories therein.

Psalms 18:47 It is God that avengeth me, and subdueth the people under me.
Psalms 18:48 He delivereth me from mine enemies: yea, thou liftest me up above those that rise up against

me: thou hast delivered me from the violent man.
Psalms 18:49 Therefore will I give thanks unto thee, O
LORD, among the heathen, and sing praises unto thy
name.

This chapter gives the account of David, one the greatest Kings of Israel. Before he became King, David's life from a shepherd boy to King Saul's aid to Commander of his army, was punctuated by fear and uncertainty. He was often on the run from the envy and jealousy of the King. In this chapter, he begins by pouring out his praises to God giving several reasons why. Fast forwarding to the forty seventh verse through the forty ninth, he underscores how God avenged him and subdued people under him. He narrates how the Lord had delivered him from his enemies and lifted him above those that rose up against him. He concludes by saying, 'therefore will I give you thanks and sing praises'.

Child of God, what lessons do you draw from this passage? Everything in the Bible was written for our example. We are instructed to praise God for avenging us of our enemies. The life and story of David should inspire you to take stock of all the occurrences of your life and to learn to package them in a such a way that you give praise to God for outwitting and overthrowing the plans of the Devil in your life. What are you waiting for, put the book down and begin praising Him for avenging you in that area of life. You will never comprehend the blessing and benefits emanating from a life of gratitude and thanks to God.

Chapter Six

For His Creation

In our final chapter we focus on Man, the greatest masterpiece and invention of God. Created in God's image and after His likeness, Man was given ruler-ship and dominion over all the works of God. He is God's representative and vice-regent in this realm. God cannot interfere in the affairs of the earth without His representative's permission. Psalms 115:16 The heaven, even the heavens, are the LORD'S: but the earth hath he given to the children of men. This permission is granted when we beckon God in our prayers for His Kingdom to come and His will be done.

Taking a close look at the morphology and structural design of God's greatest design, man, you will discover there is a lot one should take note of. The Psalmist helps paint a vivid picture of God's model and in his citation he declares it a valid reason to praise God. Let us examine the scriptural reference.

Psalms 139:14 I will praise thee; for I am fearfully and wonderfully made: marvelous are thy works; and that my soul knoweth right well.

The whole of Psalm 139, is devoted to Man. It describes the State of the art of the manufacturer's model. In it, David pauses and makes this poetic utterance, 'I will praise you for I am fearfully and wonderfully made'. Whereas God in the first five days of creation spoke the universe and everything in it into being; the creatures of the waters, birds of the air, the diverse animal and plant species and entire galaxy, when it came to creating Man on the sixth day, He consulted with 'himself' saying, 'let us make Man in our image, after our likeness'. It was a diligent work that required time and precision. The carefulness and artistry put into fashioning Man was un-comprehendible. The only creation that is a spirit being, capable of living forever! The bible declares, 'Even before you were ever formed in the womb, I knew you and planned for you'.

The psalmist goes on to describe how His wonderful plans and purposes for our lives are un-imaginable.

You and I go through life apprehensive about today and tomorrow, not knowing your life's manual was already written and shelved in His eternal mind. The proof of His eternal love is seen in the way He archives precious thoughts for every single one of us. He makes it rain on the good and bad. And like a massive library, God's infinite mind houses records about our past, present and future. One of the ways we access this 'great library' is through our praises. When in His presence, His mind is opened to us, we begin seeing and hearing tiny bits of His wonderful plans about our families, health, prosperity, children, careers, etc.

Friend, that is why David, the sweet Psalmist of Israel penned this down. He used his life as a prototype of all humanity. Sharing his life's journey from a simple insignificant shepherd boy to one of the greatest Kings Israel, David pointed out these facts with a heart of gratitude.

Everyone of us has a life story and in our journey, God has already earmarked key points of progression and a grand finale. The reason David had this revelation about himself as a master piece of God was because of his continuous sneak peeks into the great Library, the mind/heart of God. His consistent life and habit of praise warranted him a red carpet into the mind of God, thereby revealing divine mysteries about his life. Dear reader, I wish to inspire you to understand the purpose and value of the ministry of Praise.

In the fourteenth verse of Psalms 139, David makes known to us another reason of praise. We praise God because we are fearfully and wonderfully made. In the subsequent verses, he tables varied reasons and concerns why.

From now on, take time in your praises to thank God for YOU, how special and unique you are in His eyes, how He calls you by name, has you engraved on the palms of his hands. Isaiah 49:16 Behold, I have graven thee upon the palms of my hands; thy walls are continually before me. How he will never leave nor forsake you. I can go on and on citing examples from God's word concerning His purpose for you. But I want you to get a personal revelation and make a self discovery, beginning with the passage below. In addition, start drawing from other scriptures and through them gain knowledge of how to praise and worship God for YOU. As you do, the merits will be huge as you keep practicing this culture of praise.

Psalms 139:14 I will praise thee; for I am fearfully and wonderfully made: marvellous are thy works; and that my soul knoweth right well.

Psalms 139:15 My substance was not hid from thee, when I was made in secret, and curiously wrought in the lowest parts of the earth.

Psalms 139:16 Thine eyes did see my substance, yet being unperfect; and in thy book all my members were written, which in continuance were fashioned, when as yet there was none of them.

Psalms 139:17 How precious also are thy thoughts unto me, O God! how great is the sum of them!

Psalms 139:18 If I should count them, they are more in number than the sand: when I awake, I am still with thee.

Psalms 8:4 What is man, that thou art mindful of him? and the son of man, that thou visitest him?

Psalms 8:5 For thou hast made him a little lower than the angels, and hast crowned him with glory and honor.

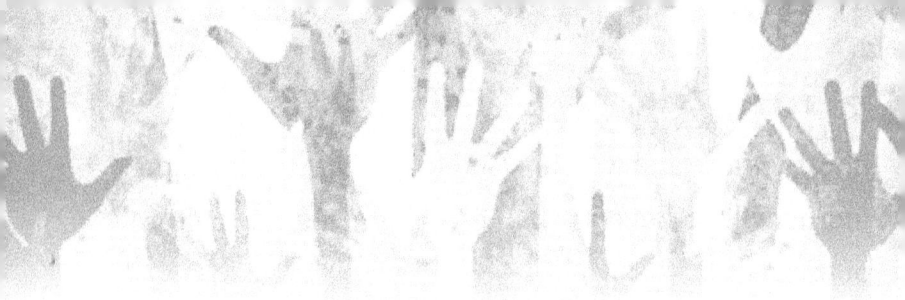

Conclusion

Our journey through the six chapters of this book has been to discover the reason as to why we Praise. Citing various scriptures to back our deposition, we have learnt that Praising God is and should be an integral part of every Christian. The personal quiet times set with God should be kick started and mingled with praise AND the public gatherings for worship should be taken with uttermost seriousness. God says, I love those who love me, and those who seek me shall find me. I believe the best way to demonstrate your love for Him is through praise and worship. So that when time comes to 'seek' Him through petition and intercession He has already been found through your Love. My heart's desire is to see an end-time praise and worship army rising up to re-claim the territories the enemy has unlawfully occupied: our health, families, communities and regions. I am talking about annihilating those false spirits that crave the worship belonging to God, and restoring the fallen tabernacle of David in our children, homes, marriages and communities. Time is of the essence, rise up and begin marching around the 'Jericho' of your finances, loved ones, job, family and neighborhood with a projected trumpet of praise, which is the fruit of your lips. Remember, around your Jericho, it is your praises that lead the way. And as you make it a consistent practice every morning when you rise up AND in the night before you tuck yourself in bed, since you have nothing to lose and everything to gain, those steep, elevated, fortified and surrounding walls are going to come crumbling and tumbling down. Praise the Lord!

Benediction

Psalms 107:8 Oh that men would praise the LORD for his goodness, and for his wonderful works to the children of men!

Psalms 107:9 For he satisfieth the longing soul, and filleth the hungry soul with goodness.

Psalms 107:10 Such as sit in darkness and in the shadow of death, being bound in affliction and iron;

Psalms 107:11 Because they rebelled against the words of God, and contemned the counsel of the most High:

Psalms 107:12 Therefore he brought down their heart with labour; they fell down, and there was none to help.

Psalms 107:13 Then they cried unto the LORD in their trouble, and he saved them out of their distresses.

Psalms 107:14 He brought them out of darkness and the shadow of death, and brake their bands in sunder.

Psalms 107:15 Oh that men would praise the LORD for his goodness, and for his wonderful works to the children of men!

Psalms 107:16 For he hath broken the gates of brass, and cut the bars of iron in sunder.

Psalms 107:17 Fools because of their transgression, and because of their iniquities, are afflicted.

Psalms 107:18 Their soul abhorreth all manner of meat; and they draw near unto the gates of death.

Psalms 107:19 Then they cry unto the LORD in their trouble, and he saveth them out of their distresses.

Psalms 107:20 He sent his word, and healed them, and delivered them from their destructions.

Psalms 107:21 Oh that men would praise the LORD for his goodness, and for his wonderful works to the children of men!

Psalms 107:22 And let them sacrifice the sacrifices of thanksgiving, and declare his works with rejoicing.

Psalms 107:23 They that go down to the sea in ships, that do business in great waters;

Psalms 107:24 These see the works of the LORD, and his wonders in the deep.

Psalms 107:25 For he commandeth, and raiseth the stormy wind, which lifteth up the waves thereof.

Psalms 107:26 They mount up to the heaven, they go down again to the depths: their soul is melted because of trouble.

Psalms 107:27 They reel to and fro, and stagger like a drunken man, and are at their wits' end.

Psalms 107:28 Then they cry unto the LORD in their trouble, and he bringeth them out of their distresses.

Psalms 107:29 He maketh the storm a calm, so that the waves thereof are still.

Psalms 107:30 Then are they glad because they be quiet; so he bringeth them unto their desired haven.

Psalms 107:31 Oh that men would praise the LORD for his goodness, and for his wonderful works to the children of men!

Psalms 107:32 Let them exalt him also in the congregation of the people, and praise him in the assembly of the elders.

Psalms 107:33 He turneth rivers into a wilderness, and the watersprings into dry ground;

Psalms 107:34 A fruitful land into barrenness, for the wickedness of them that dwell therein.

Psalms 107:35 He turneth the wilderness into a standing water, and dry ground into watersprings.

Psalms 107:36 And there he maketh the hungry to dwell, that they may prepare a city for habitation;

Psalms 107:37 And sow the fields, and plant vineyards, which may yield fruits of increase.

Psalms 107:38 He blesseth them also, so that they are multiplied greatly; and suffereth not their cattle to decrease.

Psalms 107:39 Again, they are minished and brought low through oppression, affliction, and sorrow.

Psalms 107:40 He poureth contempt upon princes, and causeth them to wander in the wilderness, where there is no way.

Psalms 107:41 Yet setteth he the poor on high from affliction, and maketh him families like a flock.

Psalms 107:42 The righteous shall see it, and rejoice: and all iniquity shall stop her mouth.

Psalms 107:43 Whoso is wise, and will observe these things, even they shall understand the lovingkindness of the LORD.

Other Books written by Andrew Allans Mutambo:

1. Four Faces of a Worshipper.
2. Worship Keys for Worth-full Living.
3. Gates of Worship.
4. Purpose of Praise.

Coming Soon:

1. Dynamics of God's Word.
2. Nine Elements of Worship.
3. Composition of Worship.
4. Principles of Faith.
5. Seven Locks of the Anointing.
6. Seven Characteristics of Prayer.
7. Seven Significances of the Cross.

www.ingramcontent.com/pod-product-compliance
Lightning Source LLC
Chambersburg PA
CBHW060614030426
42337CB00018B/3061